A Visit To The Asylum For Aged And Decayed Punsters

Oliver Wendell Holmes

[ZHINGOORA BOOKS]

A VISIT TO THE ASYLUM FOR AGED AND DECAYED PUNSTERS

Having just returned from a visit to this admirable Institution in company with a friend who is one of the Directors, we propose giving a short account of what we saw and heard. The great success of the Asylum for Idiots and Feeble-minded Youth, several of the scholars from which have reached considerable distinction, one of them being connected with a leading Daily Paper in this city, and others having served in the State and National Legislatures, was the motive which led to the foundation of this excellent charity. Our late distinguished townsman, Noah Dow, Esquire, as is well known, bequeathed a large portion of his fortune to this establishment— "being thereto moved," as his will expressed it, "by the desire of *N.*

Dowing some public Institution for the benefit of Mankind." Being consulted as to the Rules of the Institution and the selection of a Superintendent, he replied, that "all Boards must construct their own Platforms of operation. Let them select *anyhow* and he should be pleased." N.E. Howe, Esq., was chosen in compliance with this delicate suggestion.

The Charter provides for the support of "One hundred aged and decayed Gentlemen-Punsters." On inquiry if there way no provision for *females*, my friend called my attention to this remarkable psychological fact, namely:

THERE IS NO SUCH THING AS A FEMALE PUNSTER.

This remark struck me forcibly, and on reflection I found that *I never knew nor heard of one*, though I have once or twice heard a woman make a *single detached* pun, as I have known a hen to crow.

On arriving at the south gate of the Asylum grounds, I was about to ring, but my friend held my arm and begged me to rap with my stick, which I did. An old man with a very comical face presently opened the gate and put out his head.

"So you prefer *Cane* to *A bell*, do you?" he said—and began chuckling and coughing at a great rate.

My friend winked at me.

"You're here still, Old Joe, I see," he said to the old man.

"Yes, yes—and it's very odd, considering how often I've *bolted*, nights."

He then threw open the double gates for us to ride through.

"Now," said the old man, as he pulled the gates after us, "you've had a long journey."

"Why, how is that, Old Joe?" said my friend.

"Don't you see?" he answered; "there's the *East hinges* on the one side of the gate, and there's the *West hinges* on t'other side—haw! haw! haw!"

We had no sooner got into the yard than a feeble little gentleman, with a remarkably bright eye, came up to us, looking very serious, as if something had happened.

"The town has entered a complaint against the Asylum as a gambling establishment," he said to my friend, the Director.

"What do you mean?" said my friend.

"Why, they complain that there's a *lot o' rye* on the premises," he answered, pointing to a field of that grain—and hobbled away, his shoulders shaking with laughter, as he went.

On entering the main building, we saw the Rules and Regulations for the Asylum conspicuously posted up. I made a few extracts which may be interesting:

SECT. I. OF VERBAL EXERCISES.

5. Each Inmate shall be permitted to make Puns freely from eight in the morning until ten at night, except during Service in the Chapel and Grace before Meals.

6. At ten o'clock the gas will be turned off, and no further Puns, Conundrums, or other play on words will be allowed to be uttered, or to be uttered aloud.

9. Inmates who have lost their faculties and cannot any longer make Puns shall be permitted to repeat such as may be selected for them by the Chaplain out of the work of *Mr. Joseph Miller*.

10. Violent and unmanageable Punsters, who interrupt others when engaged in conversation, with Puns or attempts at the same, shall be deprived of

their *Joseph Millers*, and, if necessary, placed in solitary confinement.

SECT. III. OF DEPORTMENT AT MEALS.

4. No Inmate shall make any Pun, or attempt at the same, until the Blessing has been asked and the company are decently seated.

7. Certain Puns having been placed on the *Index Expurgatorius* of the Institution, no Inmate shall be allowed to utter them, on pain of being debarred the perusal of *Punch* and *Vanity Fair*, and, if repeated, deprived of his *Joseph Miller*.

Among these are the following:

Allusions to *Attic salt*, when asked to pass the salt-cellar.

Remarks on the Inmates being *mustered*, etc., etc.

Associating baked beans with the *benefactors* of the Institution.

Saying that beef-eating is *befitting*, etc., etc.

The following are also prohibited, excepting to such Inmates as may have lost their faculties and cannot any longer make Puns of their own:

"——your own *hair* or a wig"; "it will be *long enough*," etc., etc.; "little of its age," etc., etc.; also, playing upon the following words: _hos_pital; *mayor*; *pun*; *pitied*; *bread*; *sa uce*, etc., etc., etc. *See* INDEX EXPURGATORIUS, *printed for use of Inmates*.

The subjoined Conundrum is not allowed: Why is Hasty Pudding like the Prince? Because it comes attended by its *sweet*; nor this variation to it, *to wit*: Because the *'lasses runs after it.*

The Superintendent, who went round with us, had been a noted punster in his time, and well known in the business world, but lost his customers by making too free with their names—as in the famous story he set afloat in '29 *of four Jerries* attaching to the names of a noted Judge, an eminent Lawyer, the Secretary of the Board of Foreign Missions, and the well-known Landlord at Springfield. One of the *four Jerries*, he added, was of gigantic magnitude. The play on words was brought out by an accidental remark of Solomons, the well-known Banker. "*Capital punishment!*" the Jew was overheard saying, with reference to the guilty parties. He was understood, as saying, *A capital pun is meant*, which led to an investigation and the relief of the greatly excited public mind.

The Superintendent showed some of his old tendencies, as he went round with us.

"Do you know"—he broke out all at once—"why they don't take steppes in Tartary for establishing Insane Hospitals?"

We both confessed ignorance.

"Because there are *nomad* people to be found there," he said, with a dignified smile.

He proceeded to introduce us to different Inmates. The first was a middle-aged, scholarly man, who was seated at a table with a *Webster's Dictionary* and a sheet of paper before him.

"Well, what luck to-day, Mr. Mowzer?" said the Superintendent.

"Three or four only," said Mr. Mowzer. "Will you hear 'em now—now I'm here?"

We all nodded.

"Don't you see Webster *ers* in the words cent_er_ and theat_er_?

"If he spells leather *lether*, and feather *fether*, isn't there danger that he'll give us a *bad spell of weather*?

"Besides, Webster is a resurrectionist; he does not allow *u* to rest quietly in the *mould*.

"And again, because Mr. Worcester inserts an illustration in his text, is that any reason why Mr. Webster's publishers should hitch one on in their appendix? It's what I call a *Connect-a-cut* trick.

"Why is his way of spelling like the floor of an oven? Because it is *under bread*."

"Mowzer!" said the Superintendent, "that word is on the Index!"

"I forgot," said Mr. Mowzer; "please don't deprive me of *Vanity Fair* this one time, sir."

"These are all, this morning. Good day, gentlemen." Then to the Superintendent: "Add you, sir!"

The next Inmate was a semi-idiotic-looking old man. He had a heap of block-letters before him, and, as we came up, he pointed, without saying a word, to the arrangements he had made with them on the table. They were evidently anagrams, and had the merit of transposing the letters of the words employed without addition or subtraction. Here are a few of them:

TIMES. SMITE! POST. STOP!

TRIBUNE. TRUE NIB. WORLD. DR. OWL.

ADVERTISER. { RES VERI DAT. { IS TRUE. READ!

ALLOPATHY. ALL O' TH' PAY. HOMOEOPATHY. O, THE ——! O! O, MY! PAH!

The mention of several New York papers led to two or three questions. Thus: Whether the Editor of *The Tribune* was *H.G. really*? If the complexion of his politics were not accounted for by his being *an eager* person himself? Whether Wendell *Fillips* were not a reduced copy of John *Knocks*? Whether a New York *Feuilletoniste* is not the same thing as a *Fellow down East*?

At this time a plausible-looking, bald-headed man joined us, evidently waiting to take a part in the conversation.

"Good morning, Mr. Riggles," said the Superintendent, "Anything fresh this morning? Any Conundrum?"

"I haven't looked at the cattle," he answered, dryly.

"Cattle? Why cattle?"

"Why, to see if there's any *corn under 'em*!" he said; and immediately asked, "Why is Douglas like the earth?"

We tried, but couldn't guess.

"Because he was *flattened out at the polls*!" said Mr. Riggles.

"A famous politician, formerly," said the Superintendent. "His grandfather was a *seize-Hessian-ist* in the Revolutionary War. By the way, I hear the *freeze-oil* doctrines don't go down at New Bedford."

The next Inmate looked as if he might have been a sailor formerly.

"Ask him what his calling was," said the Superintendent.

"Followed the sea," he replied to the question put by one of us. "Went as mate in a fishing-schooner."

"Why did you give it up?"

"Because I didn't like working for *two mast-ers*," he replied.

Presently we came upon a group of elderly persons, gathered about a venerable gentleman with flowing locks, who was propounding questions to a row of Inmates.

"Can any Inmate give me a motto for M. Berger?" he said.

Nobody responded for two or three minutes. At last one old man, whom I at once recognized as a Graduate of our University (Anno 1800) held up his hand.

"Rem *a cue* tetigit."

"Go to the head of the class, Josselyn," said the venerable patriarch.

The successful Inmate did as he was told, but in a very rough way, pushing against two or three of the Class.

"How is this?" said the Patriarch.

"You told me to go up *jostlin'*," he replied.

The old gentlemen who had been shoved about enjoyed the pun too much to be angry.

Presently the Patriarch asked again:

"Why was M. Berger authorized to go to the dances given to the Prince?"

The Class had to give up this, and he answered it himself:

"Because every one of his carroms was a *tick-it* to the ball."

"Who collects the money to defray the expenses of the last campaign in Italy?" asked the Patriarch.

Here again the Class failed.

"The war-cloud's rolling *Dun*," he answered.

"And what is mulled wine made with?"

Three or four voices exclaimed at once:

"*Sizzle-y* Madeira!"

Here a servant entered, and said, "Luncheon-time." The old gentlemen, who have excellent appetites, dispersed at once, one of them politely asking us if we would not stop and have a bit of bread and a little mite of cheese.

"There is one thing I have forgotten to show you," said the Superintendent, "the cell for the confinement of violent and unmanageable Punsters."

We were very curious to see it, particularly with reference to the alleged absence of every object upon which a play of words could possibly be made.

The Superintendent led us up some dark stairs to a corridor, then along a narrow passage, then down a broad flight of steps into another passageway, and opened a large door which looked out on the main entrance.

"We have not seen the cell for the confinement of 'violent and unmanageable' Punsters," we both exclaimed.

"This is the *sell*!" he exclaimed, pointing to the outside prospect.

My friend, the Director, looked me in the face so good-naturedly that I had to laugh.

"We like to humor the Inmates," he said. "It has a bad effect, we find, on their health and spirits to disappoint them of their little pleasantries. Some of the jests to which we have listened are not new to me, though I dare say you may not have heard them often before. The same thing happens in general society, with this additional disadvantage, that there is no punishment provided for 'violent and unmanageable' Punsters, as in our Institution."

We made our bow to the Superintendent and walked to the place where our carriage was waiting for us. On our way, an exceedingly decrepit old man moved slowly toward us, with a perfectly blank look on his face, but still appearing as if he wished to speak.

"Look!" said the Director—"that is our Centenarian."

The ancient man crawled toward us, cocked one eye, with which he seemed to see a little, up at us, and said:

"Sarvant, young Gentlemen. Why is a— a—a—like a—a—a—? Give it up? Because it's a—a—a—a—."

He smiled a pleasant smile, as if it were all plain enough.

"One hundred and seven last Christmas," said the Director. "Of late years he puts his whole Conundrums in blank—but they please him just as well."

We took our departure, much gratified and instructed by our visit, hoping to have some future opportunity of inspecting the Records of this excellent Charity and making extracts for the benefit of our Readers.

End of the book.